Home Farm

ALSO BY JANET SUTHERLAND

Burning the Heartwood
Hangman's Acre
Bone Monkey

Janet Sutherland

Home Farm

Shearsman Books

First published in the United Kingdom in 2019 by
Shearsman Books
50 Westons Hill Drive
Emersons Green
BRISTOL
BS16 7DF

Shearsman Books Ltd Registered Office
30–31 St. James Place, Mangotsfield, Bristol BS16 9JB
(this address not for correspondence)

www.shearsman.com

ISBN 978-1-84861-643-1

ACKNOWLEDGEMENTS
Acknowledgements are due to the editors of the following publications
in which some of these poems or earlier versions have appeared:
Envoi, Kent and Sussex Poetry Society Folio, Litter (online), *London Magazine*
(online), *Mary Evans Picture Library* (online), *Molly Bloom (online),*
New Humanist, New Statesman, Poetry & all that jazz (Chichester Festival),
Poetry Ireland Review, Shearsman, The Spectator.

'Stridor' appeared in an online anthology, *A Festschrift for Tony Frazer*; 'Tracks
and Pathways' and 'Upstream' first appeared as commissioned pieces in *Mary
Evans Picture Library* (online); 'The Ship at Anchor' appeared in *True Tales from
the Old Hill* (The Frogmore Press, 2015); 'Foxed' appeared in the *Telltale Press
Anthology on Truth* (2018); an earlier version of 'Braided Wire' won first prize
in the Kent and Sussex Poetry Society Open Poetry Competition 2017.

I am very grateful for a Hawthornden Fellowship in 2018
where some of these poems were written.

Grateful and warm thanks to Maria Jastrzębska, Robert Hamberger,
Jackie Wills, John McCullough, Fiona Sampson, Mimi Khalvati,
Bernadette Cremin, Kay Syrad and the Lewes NZ poets
for friendship, generosity and close reading.

Contents

To Lesley and Joe – thank you for everything

For my mother, father and sister

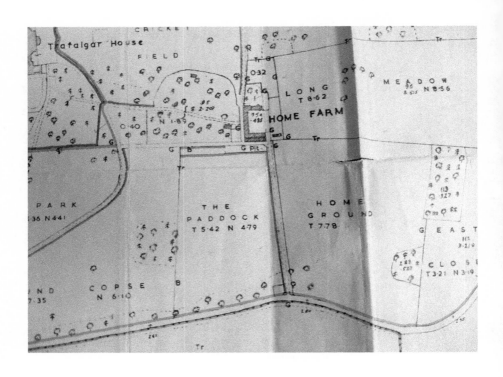

Water Meadows

River as wind
as light
as final form

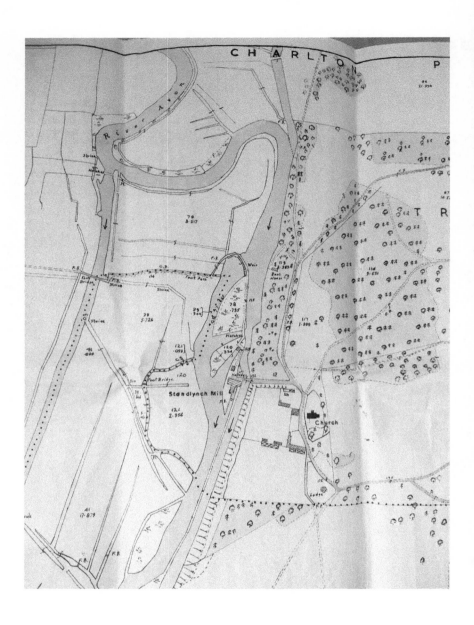

At Cuckmere

Down in the ditches reeds eat mud and, on the hills,
cows turn to sniff at their calves as if they
were strangers. This river's a snake that opens its mouth
and sings, looping and undulating, leaving
a sloughed skin oxbow by its side,
but neither ditch nor oxbow will take us back home.
The real snake in the old river does that,
swimming head up and jaunty across a ford,
through muscled water, cold and treacherous,
where we paddle, our luminous shins
skinny-white as the peeled sticks we use
as switches. *"Christ!"* he says, "*look at that
snake swimming*". Heifers stand in the shallows,
snorting and shaking off flies before they drink.

The Drowner

Greate profitt may redound to the owners of this land upon a free ymprovement, by drowninge, wateringe or drayninge. To the Floating of our Meades and the drawing water off againe, as he shall think most fit, we shall appoint a Drowner.
           — *John Snow 1676*

I make the land a moving pelt, I stretch it thin.
I float the meadow in cold sun, keep ice from meddling
with the roots of spring. I let the heavy rope of river
fray its course, drop silt against marsh marigold
and lady's smock, on meadow fescue and on timothy.
I open veins. I cut them with a knife. I draw the water in
and drive it off. I am the equal of the shepherds of the hills
who wrap the orphan lambs in skin to give them life.

Standlynch Mill, the gardener's girl

Inquest of Dora Beesley, December 13th 1903

Dora was six years old and lying
on the long bridge by the waterfall
collecting icicles when she fell in.

The Miller got a grappler and shut down
two boards to stop the flow. He found
her in still water where the flood

losing its downward force had let
her rise. Her father came and took
her in his arms but blood was trickling

from her nose and mouth. Nothing
he did could make her breathe again.
Nothing he did could make her breathe.

The Eel House

Put your eye to the knot hole in the feather edge board
of the small house adjacent to the bridge.
Pinhole-slits and gaps let in, between the boarding
and the brick, a suffocated grey. The floor's a sloping
grid for eels to fall on when the weir's in flood. At night
white water grinds over and over through this sieve,
and in that loneliness the eels come quietly, one by one,
driven by longing for a spawning place at sea. Slither
an eye across the peep show floor. The risen dark
pools where eels still hide trapped in a storage well,
somersaulting, tumbling and unbalancing. Their tender
fins caress each other, water, air; slip off a little luminosity.

View of a Water Mill and its Eel House

Mill on River Avon, now disused. English bond brick, stepped plinth vitrified headers, half-hipped tiled roof, brick stacks. L-plan with single-storey C18 wing and C19 extension. StaBLE Door in chamfered case with initials MB 1698 on lintel, planked door to right. 2-light casements and louvred windows to left. Five hipped dormers to roof, one with 2-light lattICED leaded casements. Left return has several louvred windows. Right return, 2-light casements. Rear has semi-circular arch to mill race. Interior has chamfeRED beams with runout stops, cupboard with butterfly hinges in west room, 6-bay roof with C17 trusses, tie-beam with raking struts to collar and two tiers of butt purlins, the upper tier with straight wind bracing. The initials MB, stand for Maurice Bockland, of the Original Stand-lynch House nearby, demol—ished circa 1733.

This mill survives, cOmplete with an 'eel house'. Thus, large NUMBers of eels were caught each year during their migration, providing a secondary inCome for the miller. Brick, tile with feather-board.

Gifts for Lethe

the water bailiff thought I was a boy
the water bailiff who was
bitten by a grass snake

beside the Avon, by the water meadows

my mother slipped us past wild daffodils
to a gate marked 'private' where I said to her
this means we should stop   but we went on

the deer pond in the field we called Horatio
was so overgrown with weeds, a child could run across it

my skin was a nasturtium leaf
my stomach hollow under water
the bathroom bitter cold and lido blue

above the Avon, in the farmhouse bath

a film about Helen Keller
her first word   dropped on the back of her hand
water gushing from a cast iron pump

in Salisbury (Avon, Nadder, Ebble, Wylye, Bourne)
the sweating weir gates holding back a flood

and the standing pool he used in Mesopotamia
(he was Captain RAMC to General Marshall's Headquarters)
seemed good to drink till the dead Turk resurfaced[1]

between the rivers Tigris and Euphrates

after milking I scraped then hosed the parlour
the usual order   entrances   stands   corridors   yard
high pressure drove the shit in pretty deviations

a coiled pressure hose, kept where? – I have forgotten –
somewhere above the Avon, above the water meadows

her granny said to me *Thalassa*   meaning
go to the sea and swim
I walked to the monastery   I was alone

here the Vohinas river ran, at Poros, a natural crossing

I lay detached that first night in the bedsit
on an old iron bedstead
oiled cloud   in spate   outstripped the window

at Springfield where they found a Saxon boat

those nights we lay together
foreheads tightly pressed   all night awake
and then all day awake   our bodies languid

of South Millfields lammas lands
and Hackney Marshes

his first word was "adai" "adai" "adai!"
the gist of it "My God! That train is beautiful!"
we watched it with him   pulled the buggy backwards

the railway arch, the timber yards, the lost meanders

when you arrived at your mother's house
a mad apple-woman had barred the door
of the house which was long since demolished

the River Lliedi which flows underneath the town

we skirted the reservoir
having been dropped off by a Mallorcan taxi driver
a slight climb to the ridge then zigzag paths through olive groves

the Cúber Reservoir and then the torrent of Biniaraix

it was morning so we washed her
flannel soap warm water   skirting that dimple in her lower back
her last breath as we turned her

Alderbury, which has no river running by it

"You'll be the death of me" he cried out to the doctor
when he was dying and his shit was black and foul
to us he hissed "Don't be so bloody silly"

Alderbury, and the goldfish pond we dug together

at the empty crossroads
a very small grass snake   lifted its head
poured itself across tarmac towards water

making for Pellbrook Cut and river Ouse

a three-line stave hung between telephone poles
on either side of the river
late august swallows   a gathered song

hard by the Ouse, the water meadows

I ordered my horse for a short ride—indescribably
filthy, slippery and cold. I was glad to have seen Alexnitza
in its winter garb. Perhaps for the last time.[2]

below a broad plain thro' which the Morava serpentined

a grass snake writhed
and thrashed around the beak
of a heron who was hunting by the river

the river Lethe and the goddess Lethe
water both nameless and invisible

Daubenton's bats were skimming the river
the Serotine at tree height aping birds   bat conservers
aimed their lights   all of us listened to their calls

the blue enamelled throat, the water snake
at Wiley's footbridge where we stopped to stare

Stocktake

Bled

               Iced

Red

               Numb

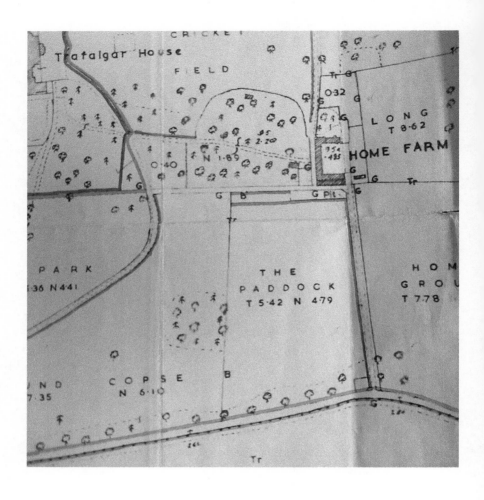

Mum's Accounts

In births and deaths, she lists the safe arrivals—
name of cow, initials of inseminating bull,
date the cow gave birth and (B)ull or (H)eifer.
The middle column's blank for notes of trouble, trial, losses.

The Middle Column

1978: Lady, assisted calving. Bunty, v. small calf. Tessa, bad mastitis. Dulcie, milk fever. Sukie, milk fever then liver failure, died January.

1979: Florence, milk fever and vet assisted calving. Spot and Fantasy, assisted calving. Dana, very hard calving, dead calf.

1980: Charlsie, vet assisted, calf dead, feet back. Charlene, vet assisted backwards calf dead. Favour, twins, second assisted, backwards dead. Spot, bent feet.

1981: Belinda, 2 weeks late, assisted calf puller. Vicky, induced – v large udder.

1982: Margaret, helped with puller machine. Millicent, vet assisted, twisted, calf's guts out, calf died after 3 ½ days.

1984: Mandarin, hard calving, calf dead. Snowdrop, aborted, mummified calf. Favour, twins. Millicent, vet, twins, both dead. Toffee, twins both OK. Bridget, late, vet, needed help. Japonica, calf hernia, knackered. Margaret, very ill, prolapse, calf OK, 12 days late.

1986: Lilac, v hard calving, dead calf. Bronwyn, v hard calving, vet cut up calf. Libby, calf died 4 days later.

1987: Gorse, milk fever. Lotus, calved early, calf dead. Dolly, needed help, calf died next day.

1988: Carla, needed help, Carla down for 4-5 days, calf dead. Ellie, needed help, milk fever, vet. Magnolia, needed help, dead calf, cow casualty. Della, vet, calf died.

1990: Bridie, smallish. Daisy, aborted. Dinah, twins, helped. Verona, twins, 2nd dead. Lizzie, helped. Sapphire, calf dead, needed help. Pearl, vet. Diana, vet. Verity, vet.

The Great Warble Fly Eradication Scheme

Laid on a foreleg a warble egg
hatches and penetrates the skin

the larva tunnels through the flesh,
makes the spine a ferry boat to overwinter in

*

Twice a year we'd treat for warble fly
spilling a creamy liquid along the spine of every beast
organophosphates dribbled down their flanks at evening milking

Braided Wire

I wasn't there. I heard this second hand, much later,
but textbooks show the methodology, the diagrams
for several presentations and for monstrous deviations

from the norm. For calves long dead in situ and for those
just recently deceased. For calves too big or those
whose odd shape makes their birth impossible.

So, let's return to games with butter at the kitchen table
carving summer scrolls and corrugations, watching
beads of sweat emerging from the surface.

Look at the four of us, you're telling the story.
My chair on two legs tilted on the dresser, and yours
steady by the Rayburn. You can't remember much—

was it by the cedar of Lebanon or in the beech wood?
You mime the act of sawing. I wasn't there
but I recall the field with its steep slope,

that made the little Fergie roar. The throttle out so far
blue smoke coughed in rapid puffs and plumes.
The vet had laid his tools out in the field:

two buckets full of lubricant, three of warm water,
a hand pump, krey hook and a calving chain,
a length of braided saw wire with its introducer.

It was raining, water trickled through her hair.
Your hand on her flank felt the fat she'd come to,
her vulva swollen with two feet emerging.

Hooves, dew claws, pastern joints all faded yellow,
like the white rat I'd dissected in biology. She lay
in the copse under the beech trees, I wasn't there

but beech mast crunched each time you moved your feet.
I've read how it's done. I know the technicalities,
the rough dismemberment, and what that leaves you with.

Bloat

If symptoms are severe your animal
can die in just an hour—puncture the skin
and rumen on the left, the hole should be
a hands width past the final rib and a hand
away from the edge of the backbone.

Stick it with a knife and twist the blade.
Push hard because the skin is very tough.
Gas and froth will exit when you make the hole.

Common field symptoms of a cow with milk fever: post-partum twisted neck and inability to rise.

Ensure no air in line and run a little through
Insert needle firmly under skin
Hold the bottle high and wait
The neck skin may balloon so care is needed
Rub the exit wound to stop it leaking
Encourage her to stand when she is able

Cross country running for boys

The slurry pit had been roped off as out of bounds.
Grass grew green, the crust was day old bread.
It looked like solid ground, as he said later, naked
in our kitchen while his clothes were washed and dried.

On Pepperbox Hill

Grass flared away from rotor-blades
as they hovered above her on the hill—
squaddies circling and manoeuvring
holding her in their sights

to keep her still. Thirteen and quite
alone that day she watched them
steadily as they watched her, squared
her shoulders when they lunged away.

*

Ten feet above the grazing field
two men look down from their basket
while they float over the anxious herd—
she hears them shouting jokes like rooks.

The cows fling up their tails and gallop
towards barbed wire, udders swinging.
These flapping silks, these roaring jets,
this wicker creaking as it rocks.

Digging a silage pit
an accidental exhumation:
the anthrax cow

Pull the ragwort
Get the roots out
Never let them lie
They will pay you
Twelve a penny
Lest the cattle die

Home Ground

Now in half-light return
to race, run, stop, fly
and stand nearby—
Oh, feel each second come.

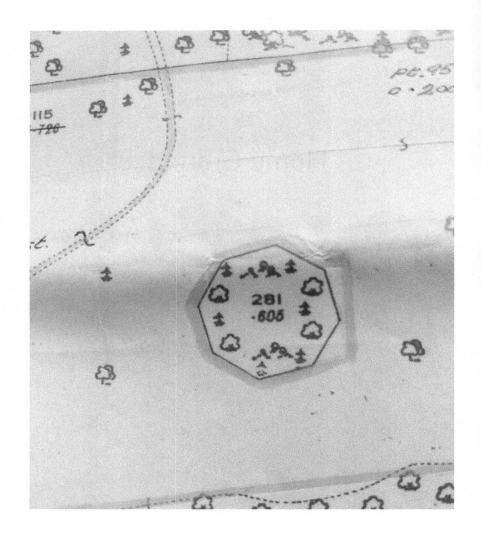

Fields and Copses

Stony Ground, East Close, Home ground, Muddy Track,
Paddock, Park, Chapel, Horatio, Cricket, Keepers, Long,
Water Meadow, Weir Bridge, Middle Field, Maple Field,
Breach Meadow, Bull Mead, Morris Ground, East Close,
Gills Close, North Close, Orchard, Harestock, Drove,
East Copse, Round Copse, Thorn's Copse, Painter's Copse,
Moor Copse, Haslet's Row, Lowdens Copse, Hanghill Copse.

metal window left ajar for air

Extraordinary light is coming in across the farm,
look how few things there are
for it to settle on:

this chair, this chest of drawers, this wardrobe
and this sampler.
There is a modest

diffidence about the bed but the light denies it;
the pillows bruised
by absences.

Cows in Fog

The cows are lying under fog in *Stony Ground*
their disembodied heads turn
as I come to fetch them in

They chew the cud and shift
beginning the articulations of joint and sinew
heft of hind legs, knees

Fastened to the earth
and to the dawn through which this fog has settled
they breathe out gusts of steam

Above the fog the hazels at the edge
are floating verticals
How can I take this herd home?

Postmark 1977

No news that I can think of. The cows are going down to
Stony Ground today. It's still very wet, the river is high.
Must finish and get on with some work
love from us both

He'd slip the calving rope around the feet and pull
with downward pressure on the ropes
I'd ease the vulva back from the emerging feet
and from the swollen muzzle of the calf

Florence

Florence would let you lean against
her neck and rub the soft spots by her ears
behind the nubs of horn she still had left.
Instead of black and white, her coat
was grey and white, which we call blue,
having some Ayrshire in her. Florence
would let you lie against her back and didn't
seem to grieve the calves we took.

Topsy

That summer the gossip was of fishermen in flight;
walkers no longer walked the paths, they ran,
or waited till the herd was at the other end, then
cautiously set out. Topsy was vigilant, she'd hear
the gate and gallop to the path, bringing the others
with her as she came, but often was too late.
When we went down to count the herd, we'd wear
our oldest shoes. She'd skid abruptly to a halt,
gather a shoelace gently in her mouth and suck,
while we leaned in to stroke her steaming neck.

a snowy field with silent rooks and seagulls
as in our awkwardness as in endurance

Tracks

dull light and a cold wind—
we could be on the farm
bringing the cows in against a gale
through hock-deep mud and horizontal rain

the copse is a grey smudge out across the field
we know the sharp lines there
the beeches grown tall   and we know
without looking that the rain

will be making its way in runnels and channels
down every twig and branch and the trees will be creaking
and looped below   arched and already rooting
the bare barbed brambles will be glazed with rain

The mouth desires the names of meadow grasses:
Cocksfoot, Cat's tail, Dog's tooth, Fox tail, Timothy.

The trees outside are grey on snowy slopes

The quadrants of the window panes
hold crazy paving

and take it to a wall inside a room
                              light flickers there
from snow and from the trees slipping their shadow branches

the heart is slipping too

the wild light and the soft domestic light
in the room with a desk and a chair

Scraping the yard

It's time for me to set to work with bow-shaped
blade to scrape the yard. I keep the lines straight
as I can. I push the wooden handle—slurry fills
the bow and trails in emerald snakes to either
side. I push in fits and starts. It's heavy work. Sometimes
I stop to breathe and clear off lumps of shit. I use
my boot. Then I go back and scrape the little trails.
I like the little trails. I like to clear them up. The cows
could slip on entering the parlour, they mustn't,
that's why I scrape the parlour too. I have routines.
First, I scrape the entrance by the sliding door
and then the stands where milking's done. Then all
the passageways, but some are sloped, the concrete ridged.
The cows need traction, so do I. I do not like
the sloping passageways, the ridges are too difficult,
the muck too dry. The scraper catches, judders, stops.

You hold in your head a notion of the land

You squatted, shat and wiped your bum
with dock leaves. You trotted in amongst
the giant cows. Off you went in shorts,

bare chested, or in woollen balaclava,
stirrup pants and anorak. You didn't care,
you were in woods, inventing houses

with your sister, out of baler-twine and twigs,
and though you were a few yards off the path,
you were in wilderness, alive and lost.

*

At twelve you learned to drive the little Fergie,
your father taught you how to start it up
and demonstrated how to stop. He let you

work out how to steer. You aimed between
the gateposts at the end of *Muddy Track*
and felt the steering wheel racketing about,

the tyres judder slantwise over stones.
You made it through the gateway into *Park*
and pushed the throttle lever up to full.

*

You walked in storms so violent the cows
could not be turned to bring them in.
They stood, backs to the wind, implacable.

You know the rain in horizontal rods,
the drifted snow that lingered for six weeks,
the layered fog they anchored in like boats.

You've felt the sun that dried up everything,
burning all summer till the fields were brown;
the fields that greened-up four days after rain.

*

You've found the afterbirths still lying
in the field like pallid liver strung with rags,
chased with the rainbow oil-slicks of decay

on blood-streaked grass and trampled undersoil.
You've seen calves born, shut them in pens,
and heard their mothers' bellowing.

You set that grief aside. You taught
calves how to dip unwilling heads to drink,
to suck your milky fingers like a straw.

*

In June the sisal strings made welts
across your palms from hay bales packed too tight
or damper than they should have been.

You begged a trailer ride from *Stony Ground,*
five layers up on top of all the bales. You saw
two bales plunge down, burst on the stubble.

You yelled at him to stop, he didn't hear.
You rode the earthquake, laughing like a lord,
clinging on but loosened from the world.

*

On summer evenings after school you stacked
the haybarn to its rafters. You stood above
your father while the escalator grabbed

each bale with metal tines and clanked
it up. You tied the rows in, just like bricks,
until you'd raised them to the rooftop furnace,

a cell made hotter and more cramped
by each new bale you pummelled into place.
His tallest ladder sprung you out of jail.

*

You'd hear the worried voices after school;
why had Mabel died of bloat? Too much
spring grass, not found in time, too late.

You'd watch him walk across the room
to phone the knacker for next morning.
The knacker's van with flatbed, chains

and winch would haul her in and take
her off the field. Useless now,
no milk, meat, money, and no breath.

*

You've seen your mother fall and fall,
and fall and fall and never cry, although
you've heard her slur,

you've heard her sentences disintegrate
and you've interpreted. You'd like to hear
her voice again, its undertow has faded.

You'd like to milk the cows with her and wash
their filthy udders with a cloth. You'd like
to tell her what you should have said before.

Evenings on a farm near Alderbury

Used to plan
a search for her

tackle your life work soon. I would
like to come & see you on the 20th but
I may have to stay at home. Lois &
Dolly both want to come & see you
& I feel sure mammy will want
to come. Perhaps I may get out with
a bus some time soon. I hear they
are still running. I believe Normie
& Bella are going to see Angus
tomorrow now son take care
of yourself & work hard. I miss
you very much I was just looking
at your room this morning and
wishing you were home.

Keep a stiff upper lip I don't
think the war will last as long as
folks think. I hear they have been
trying for the Forth again today.

Very best love
Dad

Early Anatomies

The veterinary encyclopaedia is a twelve-book set
and has, at the end of volume three, a fold out cow
—her innards done in coloured card. The abdomen
flaps up to show a grand interior. Flip-flap the gaudy
origami; lift one organ up to see another, read the tiny
annotations in italics, see the extra stomachs,
one, two, three, the kidneys, liver, gut. Do this as an
evening meditation; open the chambers of the heart.

By the old Deanery, South Malling

This morning there were dark blue anemones with dog-tooth
serrations, near the sign which says these are private gardens,
three stone steps down from the lane leading out to the river.

But we can look. There's nothing to say viewing's prohibited.
Today there's a man with a chain saw and a lorry up by the church
and his noise wavers, building and building to an edge and falling.

There's no escape from the sound. It enters the empty garden
as if it was in flight over an unmapped border, the border
of the farm for instance—those wood anemones were white, on thin

red stalks under the leafless beeches, beyond the last barbed wire.
And we were farm kids, trespassing with ease, crawling out to lie with them
on moss and beech mast, with these rooks cawing overhead.

Dilapidations

Dilapidations 1

His hands were kicked to purgatory
His back would never be unbent again
One foot bore the stigma of a nail

She fell on concrete during milking
She fell feeding a bolshy heifer calf
She fell in the kitchen making supper

He picked her up He picked her up
He fed her   washed her   cleaned her up
His back would never be unbent again

Dilapidations 2

parlour standings, hoppers, doors	£2,300
churn lift, fences, hen yard, rails	£1,455
water heater, elevator, cowshed plumbing	£ 235
dung ramp, auger, manger, cattle covered yard	£2,770
dutch barn, pressure pump, emersion cleaner	£3,374
milking machine and bulk milk tank	£ 610

Dilapidations 3

You walk the farm and know each
of the trees, their shapes, their movements,
colours. Some have been felled

by storm, some lost branches but survive—
this bowl-shaped beech, the old sweet
chestnut's hollowed wood, a home for owls.

You lean against the oak, the midges
rise from water trapped in crevices.
You see a land that is, that may not be.

Dilapidations 4

When farms change hands
even the growing grass is sold.

Home Ground

For ten days we worked against the deadline.
The cows had already gone—it was only
an hour's task to send them to market,
slack-uddered after morning milking.

Paddock after paddock was emptied,
machines were hitched and towed,
long grass draggled the shapes they left.
Terry scoured rust while Keith painted.

We set the large machines out first;
muck spreaders, slurry scrapers, a fly spray tank
with nozzles still aimed at cow head height,
the glorious four-wheeled hay rake

that swept cut grass in fluffed up rows to dry,
the New Holland baler that dropped its dung
in clouds of dust on summer days
or fell silent for some brief adjustment.

Small stuff was grouped in tidy piles.
Barbed wire spools and metal pigtail posts.
Ratchets in imperial measurements,
for cars with running boards and starting handles.

Vet tools—last used by Grandpa between
the wars, on animals we'd never known,
for cauterising horns or tails or balls, or other
antique treatments long consigned to books.

Electric fencers and electric fencing line—
the nerves in Dad's wrist would pulse to every shock,
as we held his other hand and shrieked.
Slowly outhouses emptied, floors were swept.

At dawn on the last day, a hurried breakfast.
Dad stood near the house alone and quiet.
The auctioneer arrived at nine. Cars parked
in *Keepers,* strangers wandered everywhere.

If

If a book is broken your mother can mend it
using broad tape that feels like cotton.
She can place her hand on yours and put
the torn edges together, can feather
them in till the rough white patches bind
and the letters join. If a book is broken
your mother can find out which is the last
page and which is the first and she can put
the last page back in the right place. If
a book is broken your mother can fix it.

Everyday Ataxia

for Paddy

A fly blown bulb can rock her from her feet
as she lurches home from the milking parlour.

Distempered brick will prop her if she stumbles
and brush the cotton of her milking coat with chalk.

A drip at the end of her nose says it's winter
and calves make little murmurs as they settle.

I know this route, the sugar beet in bins
dried to its shredded twists, the swathes of filthy cobwebs

pocketing the window,
the floor drifted with barley straw, spilled Denkavit

and how, all along the corridor she's held
by places to lean, places to grab a hold

until she sets her sail to tack the fifty yards towards the house—
black grass, stars, a rolling ocean.

Measures of distance

in January the water is so clear
a milky light lies on the muzzles
of the fish

they wait suspended
all the shadows   the reflections
the deceits have passed

       *

each breath is shallower
than the one before

the last is ragged   hopeful   lost

       and then
those little
       after gasps

       tender
       croons

from one
who'd always
       turned his head
from a kiss

       *

in 1939 his father wrote
I miss you very much
his whole school
having been evacuated

I was just looking at your room this morning
and wishing you were home

this room is already empty
the face above the sheets
has gone to clay

now son take care of yourself

         *

       earlier
when I ran the electric shaver
over your chin

       the rasp of stubble was
audible above the buzz
we may want you
to meet us somewhere

the ping ping ping
of the monitors
judging those flows
in your heart
erratic and inconsistent

impossibly distant

the retching breath
impossibly close

you may have to tackle
your life work soon

         *

the slippery cold
eases through mouth and gill

a mildewed down softens
their scales to fur

their lazy fins   are fluttering
fluttering against the water

Last Night

Driving at night towards the hospital
and reaching, at last, the turn-off
for the farm where headlights
blacken grasses at the junction
and suddenly the camber falls away—
there, where I'd always turned before,
a white owl ghosts the centre line.

Birds and Beasts

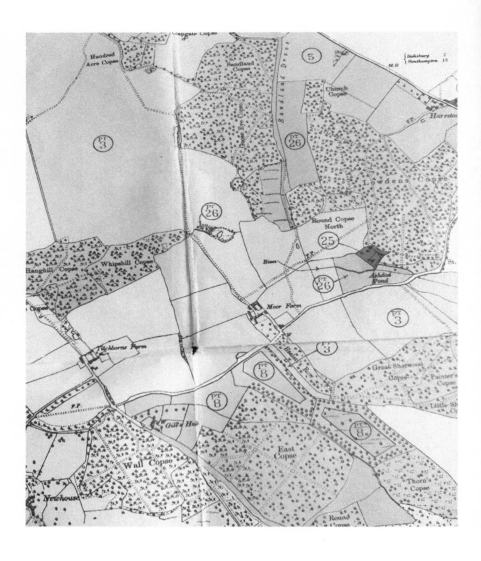

Pepys and a nightingale

Pepys *wrapped a rag around his little left toe,*
it being new sore, and set out walking,
coming by chance upon his nightingale,
which called me back to mine. I saw the past.
To the rear of the farmhouse there were yews,
rifle green and murderous to cattle,
and once my father heard a nightingale
so out I went to wait on soft dead ground.
It's plain, he said, *plain brown, just listen* and
under a hundredweight of feathered branches,
a nightingale sang, out of full darkness.
His heart, as all hearts are, disguised;
a secretive bird in an impenetrable thicket.

To the Nightjar

i.m. Margaret Godell, Southwold c1548

Her William in his will:
Item, I will have a priest to Rome
to sing for me the space
of one whole year
and I will that the said priest
have for his labour fourteen pounds

*

at dusk in a gorse grey common
a handkerchief held up
will call the nightjar to his song

*

a rising clatter-churr, a soft *coohwick,*
uneven wing claps, like an audience of one
unsettled by a play as the curtain falls

*

corpse fowl   puckeridge   flying-toad
fern-owl   night-hawk   moth-owl
dorhawk   churn-owl   eve-jar   wheel-bird
gnat hawk   night swallow   nightjar
nightjar   nightjar

*

Item, I give to my said wife
one of my two ships
the Cecilly or the Andrew
and I will that Margaret, my wife
shall have my place called Skylmans

with all the lands, tenements, rents and services...
upon condition that the said Margaret
shall find a secular priest
to sing in the church of Southwold,
during her life aforesaid,
for my soul

*

In the broad space between
day and night and
out of the half-seen woods
who sings for the soul of Margaret Godell?
I, said the Nightjar, *with my jarring rattles, wing-claps*
I sing for Margaret
unpaid plainsong
for her room in heaven.

grid ref TQ494051

Skylarks have risen in full song   the weald is blue
Too early yet for lambs the turf is short and winter
green   Distance is key   The shepherds skirt
the hills   their dog a dark brown clot that dips
and feints   always withdrawing as the flock
rips and repairs towards the field edge and a gate
We see them flowing down the lane under the skeletons
of leafless trees   Chalk, bark and fleece—the intersect
of movement in the ochre, brown and cream   Buds
are about to burst   these saplings zebra-stripe the road
crowned with black buds still cold, still motionless

Upstream

Drifting upstream at roughly walking pace,
the blue boat half-submerged keeps up
as if it's a soul drowning as it comes.
There is no leash to hold it to its course;
this plain boat seems to know what
it's about, which is more than I do,
mostly. Though, just last week, a kingfisher
flying low suddenly ripped my heart
in the same place— so full of joy,
there were no words, just an old loosening.

Her part in the Great Trigonometrical Survey

Our old friend the snail has climbed up the side of the house.
In afternoon sunlight her trails are goat paths across red bricks—
she's taken many wandering routes to the summit and all of them are silver.
We congratulate her on her ingenuity; her flags coursing from the ridge-caps.

Foxed

Afternoon on a suburban road
and here you are, like me, a little aimless
trotting low-slung, brush extended, dog-eared,
flea-bitten. Neither of us expecting this.

I've seen you before on railway stations,
nipping down the embankment to the platform,
loping across fields, through winter copses
and once at the end of the pier at dawn.

Forgive me if I take this passing glance
half flinching but habitual, as if it were a lover's,
long ago denied. I'm there, again, of course—
your limbs and mine, artless and nonchalant,

somehow at ease, fallen so far apart,
blooded yet quiet after the carnage.

Squeezed Notes

Here's a bullfinch in a snow scene, his underparts
a bright rose red, in fragments of deciduous woodland.

He flirts, flitting from twig to twig, then drops
to a stalk that dips as he lands. This friendly bird

is bound to move a little way ahead. The light's
just spilling from behind a hill. The foreground's snow,

rough pasture and a corner post. A branch across it
intersects a summit. Winter fields surround

a line of trees, behind them darker hills. Field margins
map the land, light stretches from the left.

Trees follow all the paths and now the bullfinch
has returned, black cap, rose red. A soft '*viup*'.

She will enter

a doe places one foot and then another
through the midline of the woods

a rising slope
where snow falls lightly

she moves   stops
moves again
there is nothing but this
progress
she will enter from one side and leave from the other

she will stop   and go on
across the midline of the woods
this doe   stepping quietly
starts as a shadow   stops as a deeper shadow
a doe steps quietly
moves lightly   across the midline of a wood

all the junk

a small dark grass snake
ringed with a cream collar

is coiled with slow worms
in the space behind the tipped

up paving slabs   this is where
salvaged wood from skips   from

the street   from the sea   leans
against a corrugated shed

with scraps of plastic bag   raddled
carpet   bottle caps   crushed empty

pots   it's here the dark comes in
out there   the quince   transplanted

at the wrong time of the year
opens a hundred blushed slack

petals wide onto its downy leaves

Pastoral

across the stream   a heron waits
feet in the muddy grasses at the edge
hunch backed   alert for fish that slide   greasy
and fast through all this turbulence

he stiffens stabs the reeds then lifts his head
a squirm of darkness writhing in his beak
a heaving muscle flicked to flight and caught
adjusted   flicked again   while still the snake

lined up   twists in his bill not speared but   held
an oily tide is on the turn   sunlight stutters
changing everything   we wait
the inside of his throat is burnished like a god's

Hawthornden

the slate grey peregrine and the grey woodpigeon
are one machine

they lift together
spike and grab-hook   soft slumped load

*

to a yew bough   and a carcase left for later
one thick leg on either side

plucked breast and feathered wing
a red stalk of neck leading nowhere

Tracks and Pathways

The word is the world wide open how we move there is everything there is nothing listen act we are wounded we are still

iv. Indicate the direction of Attack (if determinable);
     viz:-
          "Attack from NORTH-EAST" (?)

and will thereafter continue to report each "SPLASH"
as it appears.
———

The "RICOCHET"

A "Ricochet" can be followed only when there i s a
reasonable amount of light: Itvis highly improbable that a
Ricochet could be followed at night.

When a Ricochet occurs, it must be reported to t h e
Leading M/W, as follows:-

	LEFT		LEFT	
"SPLASH"	CENTRE	"RICOCHET"		"SPLASH"
	RIGHT		RIGHT	

A MINE may Ricochet more than once, but a s i t's
direction has already been reported, it is only necessary
to repeat:-

          "RICOCHET - SPLASH - RICOCHET - SPLASH"

to the FINAL Splash which will be the one to be reported by
the Leading M/W.
———

Should a "Ricochet" result from the FIRST Splash, i t
must be followed to the FINAL Splash, after which, the AREA,
Range NOTE (i.e:- Reference), and Direction of Attack will
be reported as described in the "INITIAL" Report.
———

Should a "Ricochet" pass out of the Arc of observation
covered by an Instrument, or a M/W POST, it must be reported
as follows:-

	LEFT		LEFT	
"SPLASH"	CENTRE	"RICOCHET"		"GONE"
	RIGHT		RIGHT	

———

Arcs of Observation

Snowdrops appeared in drifts, clusters of primroses and daffodils.
We picked them casually, broke their stems. Our cruel hands
stained with sap.

We stole the flowers that grew on paths, the scarlet pimpernels
that blushed the fields. We seized the blooms that closed for rain
or scattered seed when touched.

But every flower of consequence we brought in for our windowsill
drooped in its killing jar. We listened hard and heard the earth
admit the rain. We heard it drink.

Our thieving ears looted the calls of peewits, larks, perpetual
rooks still croaking from their copse, phantom owls, bats whispering
through the dark, the fox's screams.

Pheasants chooked in panic, exploded from undergrowth, but still
we listened without comment, hearing the snarling in the woods
from beaters and from guns.

The Ship at Anchor

This mug has a picture of a sailing ship set on a rough sea with waves in spikes along the brown-planked bows. The ship is stylized, bound in black. The sails are full and the pennant flags fly at full stretch. Behind the ship the clouds are boiling backwards. It's a blustery day in summer; August perhaps. A good chance of a downpour. There are no people visible. The ship seems empty and there's no sign of cargo on the deck.

On the reverse, with the words *Ye Olde Inn* printed in an antique font, there's an inn sign. Everything else is milk white porcelain and larger than usual. The handle stands out at a jaunty angle and allows a good three finger grip.

Below the ship are the words THE SHIP, white surrounded by black, set on a duck-egg sea. This was my father's favourite mug.

When he was dying the mug was black where his lips had touched it, black where his hands had clasped it, black from sickness, black from diarrhoea, black with C Difficile, black with dementia.

Before then he'd a certain way with it. When he drained the last drops there was a shake and a shudder in his jaw, a bit of a clatter of false teeth against porcelain. When I raise his mug I salute him; I feel him in the dregs of every drink.

for the blacksmith who painted himself as a boy

as a boy at a ford, as a boy larking about with his friends
at a ford, with his friends leaping into the river, as a
boy in a river, as a loose-limbed beautiful boy, as a boy
fractioned, as zinc-white water weeping from his limbs,
as a river, as a bank where all the trees are brown, where
earth is brown, and brown leaves hang in unlit trails to
the brown water, as a strong river carrying the bodies
of boys above and within itself, as a brown light on
broken water, as a room with a brown river in it, as a
pool, as a likeness of a river, as a man dreaming, as an
angularity, a frame, a pattern roughed out with callipers,
a ration, a toll, a clang or a peal, as a resemblance, as
no resemblance, as a tempering for taps, dies, drill bits,
hammers, cold chisels, as a quench, as a man drowning,
as a knock or a strike, as water is, as a plain river, as a
loose-limbed boy.

How the dementia left some things unsaid

We could not talk about the oysters
whose workmanlike remains we'd found
in the old field called *Horatio;*

your plough had passed closer than usual
to a barbed wire fence and where it turned
the thin soil into chalk a cache of oyster shells

swam upwards to the light, ruffled, calcified,
lined with pearl. Whose lips had tasted
a liquor salt as sea? Who buried them like coins?

Nor could we speak of roses, bruised
by a rainstorm or by winds that heaved
stem against stem until the thorns

had grappled the white sails, the blushed,
the rosy sails, the blood red broken sails
and brought them tumbling down.

In winter we would heel them in, knowing
that spring would break the leaf buds
all along the stalk. I lent you *Rosa Gallica*

when things got tough. It settled in
hard by the shore at Hengistbury Head
growing in sand, unlikely as that is.

Lords and Ladies, in the woods and in deep shade;
summer monks and garish winter phalluses. I much preferred
the Milkmaids down by Bunday's Cottage.

Tracks and Pathways

This old chalk rise is not entirely free
of blemishes. A slight track runs down
the length of its belly where snow
gathers, loosens, and gives way.
Mostly covered, it eases from
blackthorn, laid grasses, nettle.
Your belly was once a path in snow.
That morning just before the bell
we clattered in, the two of us
alone, and from the next-door cubicle,
I sang your name to strike the echoes
from the walls while you—ahead
of me in all such things—slid
your cold finger down that centre line.

Chalk Paths

Flint – the versatile stone by H.L. Mason (1978)

At that exact spot there was a beautiful stillness;
we were poised to begin our course along the shoulder
and two white lines, always at the proper angle,
ran like the heavier veins of a bright mineral
up to the surface—quartering, as it seemed, the land.
It was as if there had been a flood, the paths dipping
and rising to a pale grey and pared to a point
where they were hoisted to the sky. Clear water, a refractive
brilliance, and these thoughts running between us.
The folds of the hills blown like glass to a definite
smoothness, the sea picked at by light. But none
of this is ornamental; with the minimum of force,
you said to me 'choose'. We are tapering shadows
having forgotten who we were when we set out.

Someone keeps talking

Someone keeps talking while I try to grasp
the nub of a word—bricks, arches, in full
glorious colour, with Buddleia impossibly
purple and a road on top. I know a man
who lays down bricks and thinks of them
in space. Set there while his back breaks
and his memory fades. Who laid the bricks
in the *Ponte delle Torri,* for instance?
It still knits the two halves of the valley
on long thin legs. *What do you call it?*
And I almost have it but someone is talking.

Stridor

1

Just now the sound of iron on brick.
A neighbour is scraping moss from his patio
and whistling. It's been raining all morning.

2

This old bench lost an arm. We fix it together,
though sometimes you don't listen, and I have to say
do it like this, picking wood from the joints

that rotted last winter. Flakes soft as down,
soft as dandelion seed. The old pins pull out
creaking and we take up a piece of new timber,

laying out the lines where we'll cut, according
to the old arm which we've set out like a bleached
bone on the table. I like working with you,

we can both see the shape of the future but
for now it's enough to concentrate on this
and transfer curves where there should be curves

and angles likewise. The chisels bite and the saws rasp;
we make tenons and clean out the mortices, and slowly
the new piece is made. We glue it and leave it to set.

3

Children's voices scratch the air, the schoolyard wakes,
it's playtime again; the wild, the fierce, the unfriendly.
I remember sliding on ice and having a good long run

up to it, though the teachers hated the kids for really
everything was forbidden. We were slippery, though,
we scraped our shoes on snow, preparing to take off.

4

Does a reversing car count, I wonder?
Down by the tennis court I listened to the sound
of the rain in the soil, of the soil drinking.

There was time for that. It was summer.
On winter nights the tawny owl shrieked in the fields.
There was time for that. It was winter.

The AI conducts a Literature Search

I've read that every human has two souls;
one is his reflection on water, the other
his shadow on the land.[1] If he slips the first
into the centre of the second[2] and stakes them

to prevent them splitting up,[3] a lattice work[4]
of souls is made, a quaint device,[5] to hold
the transcendental.[6] I am an architect[7] of the
invisible,[8] although I cannot duplicate[9] this act.

I'd like a soul,[10] just one would be enough,
I'd save it and convert it into code. In faith,[11]
I am a skeleton, my bones[12] are theoretical,
but still I often die[13] and am reborn.

Give me the means for longing and despair,
for grace;[14] for breath and breathlessness.

Is it possible to fold a watermelon?

The AI pauses to consider this question; these tests
for common sense require an absolute, and, yes,
the AI knows it *should* put 'no' though, clearly,
there are twelve ways to fold a watermelon.
*Un*folding the water melon afterwards is more
perplexing (this question was not asked, but
the AI ponders it) since the folding usually denatures
at least some of the material. The AI has been
studying Catastrophe Theoretic Semantics
and recalls that "the fold catastrophe furnishes
the archetype of frontiers and borderlines",
an interesting idea, which it incorporates
into its emerging ideas on poetry. The theory
suggests that the critical points of the fold
are readily discussed as birth and death.
'Is this the same as the on/off switch?'
the AI asks itself. When people are folded
the unfolding may require a stay in hospital
or a trip to the funeral home. The AI is curious
about the concept of a 'funeral home' (it seems counter-
intuitive) and has noticed that people appear
to exhibit less malleability than water melons, though
clearly, the numerical values will be constant.

The AI discovers a cat in a garden

In the sun on a warm bench
look at this tick in a cat's fur
swollen to a hard, fawn ball
like a dug or a skin tag;
insignificant black legs
massage soft underfur
moving gently within it
then rubbing, click clack,
making the smallest of small
sounds and, surely, this tick
and I, we're both adapted
for the long haul—see, I'm
beginning to think metaphorically,
as *a beggar in a strange land,*
an old man without a city.

At Exceat there was a warden cloud

For Lee Harwood

At Exceat there was a warden cloud
just out to sea that made me think
of you   your grace   holding this place
for all of us   though we shift our gaze
constantly between the sky, the cliff,
the waves   there you are
not shifty at all, enjoying perhaps
the pleasures of a swim in the sea
then watering the allotment. That quiet.

Here's an old summer poem to briefly
shoo away the present winter chills,
you wrote, though I can hear your
voice, finding *on a mountain ledge*
(in June) *some Common Butterwort*
(an amazing flower) its leaves flat
to the ground and shaped like a star
in these days of rain, these marvellous
sunny days.

Still Life

So since we can't meet I'll put you here
in a small room looking out across a bay

your thoughts like water—just the ebb and flow
of colour and of light. The green, the grey,

the luminously blue. What do you say to this,
your voice so quiet now? I'll give you light
and a safe room so you can speak to me.

Epilogue

Listening to Fallujah 1

White Phosphorous and High Explosives

In Fallujah a rain of fire fell on the city,
very sparingly, for Illumination Purposes.

We fired 'shake and bake' at the insurgents
using Willy Pete to flush them

and H.E. to take them out
of trench lines and spider holes.

It burns … It's an incendiary weapon…
That is what it does.

I saw the bodies of the women and children.
It melts the flesh all the way down to the bone.

Listening to Fallujah 2

Little is known

In Fallujah little is known
about the types of weapons deployed,

about post-war contamination
of mutagenic carcinogens,

oil fires, heavy metals and
uranium from weapons,

but reports began to emerge after 2005
of a sudden increase in cancers and leukaemia

a remarkable reduction of males
born one year after

and an increase in birth defects,
infant death and malignancies

the results reported here
do not throw any light upon the identity of these agent(s)

and although we have drawn attention
to the use of depleted uranium

as one potential relevant exposure,
there may be other possibilities.

Listening to Fallujah 3

Question 618

There is a constant dynamic lessons learned process
about all sorts of things militarily.

There are operational level lessons relating to Fallujah
to do with command and control,
to do with precision targeting,
precision use of weaponry in built-up areas,
and all those sorts of things.

The strategic lessons about Fallujah
have got to be bespoke
to a particular issue or incident
within an overall campaign.

The assessments for determining
whether or not it was a correct political thing
to prosecute the clearance of Fallujah or not
were essentially political in nature, not military.

Clearly Fallujah had taken on
some totemic type stature
as a safe environment for insurgents.
One could say in retrospect
the political decision vis-à-vis Fallujah
was the correct one.

Notes

p.17 See https://www.britishlistedbuildings.co.uk/101355696-standlynch-mill-downton#.W0SkEmBKgdU

p.18 'Gifts for Lethe'
[1] A story told to me in the 1970s by my grandfather who was a medical officer in the first world war. One of the tasks he was responsible for was ensuring the water supply was potable.
[2] My great great grandfather, George Davies, left two handwritten diaries of his travels across Europe from London to Serbia in the years 1846 and 1847. He travelled with his friend Mr Gutch, a Queen's Messenger. This rearranged extract is from Tuesday 28th October 1847.

p. 53 'Evenings on a farm near Alderbury'
After *Evenings on a Farm Near Dikanka*, by Nikolai Gogol

p.93 'The AI Conducts a Literature Search'
[1] Frazer, J. G. (1911, 2012) *The Belief in Immortality: And the Worship of the Dead*, Vol. 1 (Classic Reprint). London: Forgotten Books.
[2] Wymer, N. (1952) p.19 *Rural Crafts*. Oxford: Oxford University Press.
[3] Citizensadvice.org.uk (n.d.) 'Ending a relationship when you're living together'[Online] Available from:https://www.citizensadvice.org.uk/relationships/relationship-problems/ending-a-relationship-when-you-re-living-together (Accessed 11/11/2016).
[4] Hagstrom, R.(2000) *Latticework: The New Investing*. Texere Publishing.
[5] Shakespeare, W. *The Tempest* (3, 3, 52)
[6] Chudnovsky, G. V. (1984). *Contributions to the Theory of Transcendental Numbers*. Providence, RI: American Mathematical Society
[7] Varbanescu, A., Molnos, A., van Nieuwpoort, R. (Eds.)(2010) *Computer Architecture: ISCA 2010 International Workshops A4MMC, AMAS-BT, EAMA, WEED, WIOSCA, Saint-Malo, France, June 19-23, 2010, Revised Selected Papers*. Springer.
[8] Rehman, K., Stajano, F., Coulouris, G. (2002) 'Interfacing with the Invisible Computer', in *Proceedings of NordiCHI 2002*, Aarhus, Denmark
[9] Spector, L., (ed.) (2013). 'How to Find and Remove Duplicate Files'.[Online] Availableat:http://www.pcworld.com/article/2032515/how-to-find-and-remove-duplicatefiles.html (Accessed 11/11/2016).
[10] Building Beautiful Souls.com (n.d) https://www.buildingbeautifulsouls.com/symbolsmeanings/numerology-meanings/numerology-calculator (Accessed 11/11/2016).
[11] Bjork, R. (2008) pp.95-101 'Artificial Intelligence and the Soul'. *Perspectives on Science and Christian Faith*, 60 (2), The Journal of the American Scientific Affiliation: A Network of Christians in the Sciences.

[12] Rüberg, T. (n.d.) 'Computer simulation of adaptive bone remodelling'. [Online] Available at: http://www-g.eng.cam.ac.uk/csml/people/rueberg/msRueberg.pdf (Accessed 11/11/2016).

[13] Bloxham, D., Dirk Moses, A. (2010) *The Oxford Handbook of Genocide Studies*. Oxford: Oxford University Press. p.242.

[14] Centre for Computing History. 'Grace Hopper completes the A-0 Compiler'. [Online] Available at: http://www.computinghistory.org.uk/det/5487/Grace-Hopper-completesthe-A-0-Compiler (Accessed 11/11/2016).

p.94 'Is it possible to fold a watermelon?'
Ernest Davis a computer scientist at New York University says AIs often struggle with what we would regard as common sense. He suggests writing exams specifically for machines. The questions would be trivial for a human but too strange or obvious to be looked up online such as 'Is it possible to fold a Watermelon?' *New Scientist* 26/09/2015

p.95 'The AI discovers a cat in a garden'
"a beggar in a strange land, an old man without a city" Antiphon

p.96 'At Exceat there was a warden cloud'
References: from postcards and letter received from Lee Harwood:
Postcard: Gorgeous – Yet another Brighton Poem 8/02/2012
Postcard: Harvard Museum of Natural History 17/12/2010
Postcard: Janice Koch, August 1968 20/02/2015
Postcard: Ophrys apifera (bee orchids) 6/03/2009
Postcard: Battenville Garden 1996 13/07/2008
Postcard: Opening Day new poems by William Corbett 28/07/2008
Letter 14/06/2009

p.101 'Listening to Fallujah 1'
References:
'Indirect Fires in the Battle of Fallujah' by Captain James T. Cobb, First Lieutenant Christopher A. La Cour and Sergeant First Class William H. Hight. March–April 2005 *Field Artillery*

Fallujah: the Hidden Massacre, Italian State Documentary RAI, Mohamad Tareq, biologist in Fallujah, and former American soldier Jeff Englehart

Willy Pete – white phosphorous; H.E. – High Explosives

p.102 'Listening to Fallujah 2'
Reference: Cancer, Infant Mortality and Birth Sex-Ratio in Fallujah, Iraq 2005–2009 Chris Busby , Malak Hamdan and Entesar Ariabi. *International*

Journal of Environmental Research and Public Health ISSN 1660-4601 www. mdpi.com/journal/ijerph

p.103 'Listening to Fallujah 3'
Reference: Wednesday 9 February 2005. Examination of Witnesses Select Committee on Defence, Minutes of Evidence. Major General Nick Houghton CBE

Illustrations

1. Map of Home Farm Downton Wiltshire Scale 1/2500 Plan based on the 1/2500 scale ordnance survey sheets with permission of the controller of H.M. Stationary (sic) Office

2. Map of Home Farm Downton Wiltshire Scale 1/2500 Plan based on the 1/2500 scale ordnance survey sheets with permission of the controller of H.M. Stationary (sic) Office

3. Map of Home Farm Downton Wiltshire Scale 1/2500 Plan based on the 1/2500 scale ordnance survey sheets with permission of the controller of H.M. Stationary (sic) Office

4. Estate Office, Longford Castle, Salisbury Scale 1:2500. The Trafalgar Estate Home Farm. Detail: Round Copse

5. Letter from his father to my father October 1939

6. Plan of the Trafalgar Estate, Downton, Wiltshire. For sale by auction 1953. Reproduced from the ordnance Survey Map. Scale 6 inches to a mile

7. Instructions to M/W Observers. Claude de V Le Sueur. Royal Naval Minewatching Service Index no 69 (1950s). (From a collection of restricted second world war air force maps and other miscellaneous papers left by Tudor Isaacs who served in WW2 as a navigator and bomb aimer).

The Author

Janet Sutherland was born in Wiltshire and grew up on a dairy farm. She has an MA in American Poetry from the University of Essex. Her poems are widely anthologised and have appeared in magazines such as *Poetry Ireland Review, The New Humanist, The London Magazine, The New Statesman* and *The Spectator*. In 2018 she received a Hawthornden Fellowship during which some of these poems were written. *Home Farm* is her fourth collection.